A CHOICE FROM TWO POCKETS

A CHOICE FROM TWO POCKETS

POEMS BY

CARLOS REYES

Acknowledgments

"Ofelia and Her Lover" was first published in *Two People in the Night by a River* (2006).

"The Spanish Poet" was first published in *The Minnesota Review*.

Cover art "Poppy Field," acrylic on canvas by Max Checkoway. Author's photo by Karen Checkoway.

Cyberwit.net
HIG 45 Kaushambi Kunj, Kalindipuram
Allahabad – 211011 (U.P.) India
http://www.cyberwit.net
Tel: +(91) 9415091004
E-mail: info@cyberwit.net

If I am only for myself, what am I?

— Hillel the Elder

Contents

for Sam Green

another bard of Cloonanaha,
in gratitude

&

for Phyllis Sheck

always with us

A CHOICE FROM TWO POCKETS

You try to recapture the sweet taste
of well water from the dipper,

the after taste of metal when you come in,
wipe sweat from your brow.

You don't remember communion
you shared: drops left by those seven coming

before you to drink from the bucket
you carried from a neighbor's well.

You think of your backbreaking
labor, the bean field, then dragging

your self back to old Mister Seger's open
flat bed truck that takes you home —

too tired when you get there to eat
cornbread even with a drop

of honey or sorghum on it.

Sharing a steel bunk with a mattress thin
as the light between shadows

of iron bars on concrete, I could almost laugh
off my own desperation at that image of what

in the army we called the stockade:
The Cross Bars Hotel. Beneath

my mattress a lump, half
a paperback western *Desperado Trail*

which I was on, 3,000 miles from home.
For three days hoosegow guest in Lake City

I kissed goodnight each lights out
Zane Grey my bedfellow's words.

By early evening I've walked
all the way from Miami,

my last meal a boloney sandwich
two days ago in the Columbia County Jail.

I make it through the door with fifty others
for a place to sleep until tomorrow, a bit to eat.

The captain herds us into the chapel,
the cold back rest of a metal folding chair

keeps me awake until I find myself
mumbling along with the herd "Our father

who art in Heaven." But there's more,
a sermonette my stomach rumbles through.

We drag into the mess hall finally.
The captain thinks we'll march toward

salvation like Christian soldiers but
he's wrong and disappointed.

After another prayer, a steamy bowl
of alleged bean soup, I say alleged

because I there's not a single bean in it.
It's liquid, hot and thin as

the mattress I'll spend the night on.

In my father's house are many mansions
— John 14:2

My father's houses were
neither mansions nor Heaven.

He built them from scrap
lumber saved from other
dwellings torn down.

I followed in his footsteps
pulling from weathered boards
rusty nails, straightening

them for re-use
as he hewed rough timbers
into wall studs and rafters,
planed thin boards into trim.

But his glory was in kerfing
as he made each cut
perfectly distanced,
at the right depth

to be able to bend a straight
piece of wood into a perfect arc —
worthy of a boatwright
making ribs for Noah's ark.

From rescued timber
he built the wing

over the small creek
which sang them to sleep

each night, his gift
to them. Before, the cabin

of two rooms held seven.
One corner of the wing

was anchored to a living
huge ash with 20 penny nails.

Even then it rocked them
as though they were babes

when the southwest
wind blew, making its music

too, a different tune, than
the one of the creek

fleeting notes of a song fading
in the wind, of fledgling

dreams ever lost.

The board and batten railroad shanty
that sheltered us,

its bowed tarpaper roof like
an overturned boat we hid under

on our first night. Without warning
came a nightmare, a locomotive

thundering right through
our small shack, an earthquake

chugging by, rattling pots and pans
from shelves, shaking us awake

from a midnight dream turned to
chaos. A Cyclops' eye

flooded the shack with light, blinding
us until the nightmare passed.

A sagging strand of barbed wire was all
that protected us from a monster

that raged past a mere six feet away,
a pencil line that barely kept us from a wider world.

Tin type images burned on my retina,
a deafening steam whistle

to this day ringing in my ears.

Drifting fine snow
pushed by east wind
should return us

to a greeting card
childhood but it doesn't —
only freezing nights,

no heat, few blankets
endless hours where
Northern Lights hung

over our railroad shack's
bedroom windows.
Psychedelic Hudson Bay

trading blankets
whose high deep distance —
beauty unbelievable —

a gift incredible
but far too far
away to warm us.

Its bark is so rough that a snake won't slither across it.

Its strong hard wood is not as elegant
as oak but just as durable.

It grows along seasonal creeks
like the one by our shack.

Stubborn as ash my father,
but he never tries felling the tree,

refuses to take it on, reckons
his axe isn't sharp enough.

won't waste his sweat, risk blisters.
Instead he saves the ash

a living support for the
northwest corner of our shack.

In winter's sou'wester
the ash draws with a tidal pull

the tip of my world up and down
rocks me into dreams.

I fish all day

all day in the rain
I fish with my father,
catch nothing.

Casting out again and again
into deep water
for *peerch* (as he called them)
or trout he dismisses
as too delicate
for his taste.

We shift from foot
to foot to keep our balance
on a timber barely floating.

Bored with fishing,
I stepped out onto the biggest log.
to roll it, birl it.

I went under like a knife,
slipped between the logs

under the water
with no way up and out.

When I found a gap I surfaced,
choking on frog spawn.

Ignoring my plight, my father baits his hook
with one more earthworm.

William Stafford, *"A Story That Could Be True"*

— for Monte, Holly, Pá, Paul

And you will spend
your life searching
for the father you never had.

You found four
they are gone
and still you search
among the palms

in the jungle, by
meandering fishing streams,
along high cutbanks of turf,

in the redundant telephone book
that reminds you of a fifth
you knew only by voice.

Shoes stuffed
with newspapers to fit,

to soak up
the winter rain

as I walked to
third grade.

My teacher
gave me

shoes that didn't leak
didn't squish,

so big
like clown shoes,

and Chinese coins —
to pay me for my shame.

The coins had holes too, but
square ones right in the center.

To me they were
exotic, thrilling

though brought here
by the boat load.

Scrap metal,
valueless

as I felt
in my charity shoes.

I spin the bucket
around like a planet in orbit
not spilling a precious drop.

In that galvanized pail
I carry home dreams
to my family from Secor's well.

Dust devils
match my pace
march me home.

A boy in a well, ready to dig to China.
A dollar for each foot of depth of the circular

well, I would be rich. The soft duff of the forest
was easy, the going good. Up to my shoulders, up to

my eyes, above me at high noon I saw a full moon
shining overhead, knew there was no way out.

For what seemed like days I waited, for someone
to let down a ladder. Instead a rope came down.

At its end a water pail for me to fill with dirt.

I'd heard about
my grandfather
wriggling his fingers

in the river
to catch catfish.
It's called noodling.

In Granby, Missouri
I tried noodling,
fingering the washing

machine wringer's rollers
though there are
no fish to be caught

in a murky pool
of old clothes
twirling around

in the tub.
I'm the catch, finding
myself noodled:

a screaming eight year old,
left arm caught
in the wringer

until my mother
kills the monster.
I'm very small

for my age, but not
that small, still
in my nightmares

I am pulled
through the rollers
flattened:

Plastic Man
of the comics

hanging out to dry like
last week's laundry.

Skeletons of poetry,
skeleton keys of poetry.

Skelligs of poetry
618 rocking steps

you climb
to get there.

Skerries of poetry
you sail through

eyes closed.

Scaries of poetry
what you are left with

your muse
slipped away

gown fluttering in the merest

breath.

Hours of fruitless writing
under your pillow

nights.

Fingers splay an instrument
a lyre, a harp producing

haunting music like
threatening wind a-

rising from far at sea.
A scream of furies

wavering in intensity
for all those outside

the bedosphere to hear.
Not a harbinger of fear

but joy
abundant.

Unrequited rage
burned in her
when he took
their child and fled.

A declaration of war
between her and men
she drafted a proclamation:
They are all the same.

The oncologist casually
labeled her with
a comment
left in the chart

at the foot of her bed:
"Patient is hirsute."
An educated woman, she
knew its underhanded backstory.

She had no chance to
scribe an estimation
of *him* who, a thief
in the night, stole

her breasts
as she slept.

Yesterday a 20 Balboa coin
arrived in the mail.

An accompanying note said:
You can't spend it.

Though I can't
take it to the bank,

can't trade Núñez de Balboa
for Andrew Jackson,

each time
I look at the coin

I cash it in
for seventy year old

memories.

Until Ireland, Panama you
were my heart.

Boa that tethers two worlds
my thoughts often return to you.

And memories flow to me
like the clouded Chagres

where, foolish innocents,
we swam with the barracuda.

A commitment
like
getting engaged:

Angela smiles and slips
the scapular
around my neck.

*Don't ever take
it off, it will protect
you, our love forever.*

I never took it off
until one day it was gone
its fibers rotted in the shower

I've all but forgotten
my lover Angela
The cloth scapular

more comforting
than the steel chain
with two G.I. dog tags

that are supposed
to last forever:
two little IDs:

one sent home
if you're killed
on the battlefield

the other with the little
nick stays with the body
crimped between

your front teeth.
I never lost them,
the metal tags

by regulation never
left my neck
didn't rust away.

Though they are gone
I haven't forgotten
them, my service number

still surfaces
from time to time.
They exist somewhere

They are forever
when young love wasn't.

Alicia, Angela,
Claudette, Judy, Sonia.

Every Blue Mooner,
each whispering

compañera of the night.
They all captured me

broke my heart.
Those memories buried

deep haven't left me yet.
From time to time

they come singing
out into the night

to haunt my sleep.

Along this seawall, that Carlos of Spain
thought was gold it cost so much to build.

Today, I have returned to Panama.

The proud French rooster
from atop the obelisk surveys

the canal de Lesseps couldn't build.
On a stone bench where Ofelia waves, begs

me to snap a photograph of her
and her boyfriend.

> Seventy years ago, on this very seawall,
> trade wind blowing,

> a lock of hair onto her face
> Veronica Lake style, Alicia posed for me.

They smile, behind his head she raises
rabbit ears, a childish comic gesture.

In the background Panama Bay,
ships school like Spanish mackerel,

waiting to pay their bags of gold
to transit Pacific to Atlantic.

In the rainy afternoon Ofelia
and her lover edge back toward Chorrillo,

pocketing the coins, thin slices
of Balboa's silver helmet,

they — not I and Alicia — look
for another bench on which to rest,

an alleyway, an empty
cardboard carton for a lovers' bed.

This morning
looking southeast

at the shore of the Gulf of Panama:
silver quarter moon

laid out flat
or is it a scythe gathering

immigrants dodging coral snakes,
fer-de-lances, and bandits

beyond in the massive Darién jungle
or hiding behind the news

like me in sun faded pages
of *El Panamá América.*

The arc of the shore has left me
I'm thinking of you

arrived at my shoulder.
I am not at all surprised

to see you here.
As I stand drinking

a glass of pleasure:
Cerveza Panamá.

I offer you a sip
but no, you shake your head

You are almost 5,000 miles
and years away.

on the outside walls, tears
with invisible fingers

at the siding, and spiky
nails screech across

window panes.
I cover my ears, half awake

to the wide screaming wind.
Out through fear in the gap

between the partially open door and
its casing, not a frame

for a picture but an icicle
triangle of blackness, slice of

asphalt too frozen to drive over
where the one light bulb

over my shoulder offers no warmth,
no illumination, no explanation, or hope

even a black mare in the arrival
of what's before me in the night, galloping

pursues me.

UNAPPEASED QUESTIONS FOR NERUDA

— for William O'Daly

What creature drinks

from the paw print

of some lost cur?

Which insect leaves its eggs

here to ripen into clouds?

Which moon stares

at its reflection

in the paw's small pond?

What happens next

to mud glued to the soul,

where is it carried?

Which larger voice

envelopes an echo

of sucking sounds

of each footfall?

I watch them fall
a row of dominoes

long as the Great Wall
flattened

all the way
to the horizon.

I'm still standing
lone sentry

atop the years.

NINETY

With nine
broad lumberjack

strides, countless
mice tip-toe

clicking footsteps
here I am:

a bull wapiti
casually striding

over giant downed
fir and spruce

or skillfully creeping
up on the sunrise

on sphagnum moss
in forests deep.

As I return from
the old volcano

see my fortress
is no log cabin

in the woods
but a cheerful

20th century
Tudor cottage.

But it is none-
the-less my castle.

When I arrive
at day's end

I wonder if I
have mis-

counted steps
I've walked

to get here —
to my home

nestled under
a grand fir,

Sitka spruce,
and hemlock.

All of them
try desperately

each season
to recreate

an old growth forest.

Each evening on the screen
scenes unroll of straws and sticks
of what is left,

of the sands beneath
foundations washed and blown away
leaving captain-less houses afloat.

Survivors shake their heads
lamenting, *this was my whole life,*
our whole existence . . . See

the blue out there,
the view, ours
that's why we built . . .

My own fragile skeleton,
sun dried wasted skin:
parchment tells a story

of how tentative are
the things we possess,
believe we control.

This whirling planet
goes on each day, each year
whether we are riding

the merry-go-round
or not.

— for Nina

My daughter loops silver
bracelets engraved with
Jewish expressions on each wrist.

On her right:
I was meant for the world.
On her left: *I was meant for dust.*

Ignoring the second saying,
mishearing the first, I thought
she said, *I was meant for the road.*

In that mistake is my life.

During the Days of Awe
I anguish over what amends
to make, asking the hard questions.

Have I made a life at the expense
of everything, at the exclusion
of others? Children, I ask

your forgiveness if this road
that chose me decades ago
pushed you from my life, if

in this selfishness I ignored you, all else
except my lust for writing: poems
which in the end leave no more

than words
dust washed away by autumn rains.

PURCHASE POEMS

— for Phyllis Sheck

. . . Existence is but a brief
crack of light between
two eternities of blackness.
— Vladimir Nabokov

At the Atlantic's door it is 8 a.m.
I scrape pieces of light

from the darkness, bright
flakes of memory or myth.

This morning's rising sun
challenges glances

back over my shoulder.
In 1954 I sailed

past Lady Liberty
into a dreamed sea: gale

force Hatteras winds, clearing
to Caribbean skies, cerulean

like the weather changing
a new life beginning.

I could give you
a lot of details, history:

of Carlos V
who built the sea wall
defending Panama,
said it must be gold
it cost so much

or de Lesseps, who came
and went, unsuccessful
in building a canal
to bridge two oceans
Atlantic and Pacific.

Or me, who also came
to this place and left it,
its absence
a place buried
deep in my heart:

My phantom limb.

His will states

that a smooth

slate be set

as his headstone.

And sheltered

in front of it

a felt eraser

a box of chalk

sticks.

If you want to erase

his birth, his death

you can —

You can

change his name.

Give him

when though years or centuries

dead:

a new existence.

Li Po, "Taking Leave of a Friend"

The bobcat suddenly appears again
this side of the flower bed

ringing Phyllis' backyard.
Fire flies seek mates

in evening darkness
4th of July sparklers.

Birds from dawn
to dusk in profusion

gather at the feeder
in celebration, a hope

the new homeowners
take up where she left

off, offer seeds
of our redemption.

A sleek coat of rain
on the deck, last night's

storm soon forgotten
in morning brightness.

Mourning doves
punctuate the last few days

of her long summer.

I'm not saying
it was a Noah flood even
though I saw whole gardens
washed out
onto the pavement,

horses
eating apples
on the yellow line
of the highway.

I'm asking to borrow
your ladder.

I'm dying
to see
what's in
the '67 sedan

lodged
in the top branches
of the cork oak
along the flooded road.

And you lie there
eyes wide as the dark
night sky unable
to return to dreams.

Waiting
waiting for a pathway
to open to them but

something ineffable keeps you
awake.

Awake you think
it is a tick
of the clock, somehow
its heart has stopped

dead
dead, there is no wind
tonight, no tidal rush.

You are abandoned

abandoned to what
the house whispers.

On these foggy mornings my mind
takes a rake to a wilting garden

hoping to dig up a few dried pods
of intuition from a memory of being

abandoned by lovers so crystal clear
when at any given moment all else is erased.

The crumbling walls echo a promise
to a cottage now a shell.

A horse drawn hay mower I left to rust, a half-door
barely hanging by a lamenting hinge.

Not the song of a door flailing in the west wind
but late at night or before dawn surely

tumbling stones sing their own song
heard only by me who once made

a promise I never kept: guilt
like molding rotten leather of a horse collar

to this day tight around my neck.

> *. . . Death wooed us*
> — Louise Glück

Like the full moon dying
in its final west, trapped

in the arms of a golden tree
turned skeletal overnight.

The night before
she came to me,

fear walking fear and
frightened as I was

I made love to her.
Once again this morning

a full moon wakes us, already
a troubling blood orange.

Not much of a Thanksgiving
holiday left to celebrate,

after the news
of a former wife's death.

In quietude after so much
celebration deserted the house.

Death has it arms around us
now, as sure as the moon is

trapped in the golden tree's arms.

I.

A Greek chorus surrounds me:

village women expectant,

demanding I save the toddler

that has fallen

into the creek.

I am eleven

and ill-prepared. They beg me

to bring back

the baby's breath.

I am I left

with this life or death responsibility,

where the men are suspect

off in the fields working

or at the tavern.

I can't save him

they never forgive me:

I am left with a gift, guilt

a weight I carry, for years,

carry still.

II.
My sister Nancy was marked
for death by water
at an early age, broke
though the ice we skated on,
into the brown waters
of the Smoky Hill River.

Our older sister saves her
while I stand frozen, helpless.

III
As a young bride
she almost drowns again
tumbling into icy
Coast Range snow melt
where I dive in to rescue her
fail, almost drowning myself.

The groom watching and laughing
from shore never forgives me for my failure
but waits until the very last minute
before he finally puts down his beer
and jumps in to save her.

IV
In Alaska
the small plane
flying in weather
when no one should be flying
crashes
into the frigid waters
of Stikin Strait
well out of reach this time
of my thin arms, too distant
for them to blame me.

In Ireland the weather is always good for a funeral.
— Tony Curtis

The crow-humped old
bachelor in a worn wool jacket

barely makes his way
through the head stones,

badly-spaced substitutes
for a crutch or a stick.

His eyes failing
the persistent moss

or the ever present mist
fogging over the pertinent

dates of some friend
or relative.

Where we filed away
our ancestors.

He rubs a coat sleeve
over his stubbled chin

the hay meadow
scythed decades ago.

When we wake her this morning
her thin and red rimmed eyelids

tell us she's been
sleeping in,

protecting a none too
peaceful rest.

She dozes off
in afternoon sun.

I don't want to see
that day we know is coming.

The family discusses
her breathless existence.

They whisper
as she leaves the room.

From sun to moon
it travels great distances
lights our darkest night.

It moves in an unerring
way, captures us,
revives us,

finds its way to
our eyes opening
the tightest sewn lids.

Though camels can't,
it can pass through the
eye of a needle

burning invisible
thread, it flies through
a razor thin gap,

finds a pinhole
to escape though.
It can penetrate glass,

plunge through water
though bent
to a prismatic effect.

Through water
in a glass: a rainbow.

A raccoon snoozes
away the afternoon
in her own world.

The crotch
of a large magnolia
forms a cupped hand,

perfect daytime bed
for a creature
that no doubt dreams

of another world
not ours, yet
has no interest in it.

The giant sequoia
in the corner
of our fenced off world,

a higher safer retreat
in the neighbor's tree
she ignores

though it is hers
for the asking.

You may go up for a few days in space,
but when you return it's the same old place
— P.F. Sloan, "Eve of Destruction"

Sword-crossed vapor trails

in the eastern blue sky

leave the belly of an

ocean overhead scarred.

What we know

about all this is more

than metaphor, some

where ahead

of these chalkings

are airplanes full

of early morning

travelers dying

to escape their hum-

days-drumming.

A facile deception
as they fly

like birds, the real
pioneers of aviation,

thousands of miles
north or south.

Down here the absence
of the plane's passengers

is barely noticed.

Crumbling cork
from a bottle
of cheap champagne
barely afloat

in a vast sea
of others, bobbing
stoppers all the way
to sunset's horizon.

On one hand, the Spanish poet
he says the poor are so poor
that they don't remember —
that they are not remembered.

On the other, he says
that they die
like stones crumbling
in the Great Wall of China.

At the station
he hopped down
onto the live tracks
like a crow.

And back up again
sat on the bench,
lighted and smoked
the long butt

he found
between the tracks
didn't have time
to finish.

The west bound
train was dangerous,
ten minutes early.

— On Emma's Day

Standing at the kitchen sink
this morning
I emptied my tea cup.

A flicker of light
caused me to turn.

The sun rising — the light
just right-reflecting so clearly

she was there
in the dining room

an image fading.

The Empty Chairs of February (2024)

The Four Hinges of the World (2023)

Osage Elegy (2021)

The Ebbing Tide (2021)

Lament for Us All (2021)

Sea Smoke to Ashes (2020)

Along the Flaggy Shore (2018)

Guilt in Our Pockets: Poems from South India (2017)

The Keys to the Cottage: Stories from the West of Ireland (2015)